THINK OF THE GIGANTIC 'GLADES
NEAR THE END OF LAND...

A mama alligator floats babies on her back.

An itchy black bear takes a palm tree scratch,
    leaving soft fur tufts that swamp mice fetch.

Seminole women trailing patchwork skirts
    reach across chickee floors. They loosen
    sleep hammocks swung from cypress poles.

Cloth smiles unfurl and start to sway
    as a frog chorus swells with night hiccups.

A mother settles children to sleep
    with a sing-song Memory
    learned in the language of long ago.

She Sang Promise

The Story of Betty Mae Jumper, Seminole Tribal Leader

by Jan Godown Annino

illustrated by Lisa Desimini

afterword by Moses Jumper, Jr.

SCHOLASTIC INC.
New York Toronto London Auckland
Sydney New Delhi Hong Kong

INDIANTOWN, FLORIDA, CIRCA APRIL 1923

Spring breezes tickle cabbage palm spikes
in a woman's birth camp of the proud
Tiger Family in the powerful Snake Clan.

Fresh air carries the song of a newborn girl.
She sings promise in her cry.

The baby, born in the wild heart of Florida,
daughter to Seminole Medicine Woman
Ada Tiger, granddaughter to Seminole
Medicine Woman Mary Tiger, is
Betty Mae Tiger.

etty Mae's grandmother, Mary Tiger, sings
to Betty Mae of brave Ancestor deeds.

The women sing stories about
greed, stealth, health, and speed,
of panther, rabbit, swamp mice, and snake,
from the time when all the animals talked.

Betty Mae is a little girl at play
in the Old Everglades when
her grandmother selects
a Seminole name to guide the girl.

Mary Tiger sings the name: *Pa-Ta-Kee*.

The father of Betty Mae is a Frenchman who traps animals for pelts in the Everglades. From Betty Mae's first sing-song days, Tribal Elders force the father away. They say he has bad spirits: *Ho-la-wa-gus*. What's more, the Tiger family blends a new Mission faith with Tribal Medicine ways.

Now—one afternoon, a noisy black truck bumps into view. Elders have come for Betty Mae to throw her bad spirits into the swamp!

There is shouting. Great-uncle Jimmie Gopher brandishes his rifle. He forces the men to roar off without Betty Mae.

etty Mae is five years old when she watches
a truck leave, with chickens, cats, her dog,
bear blankets, grinding bowls, and fishing
poles. The family is moving to safety.

Dania Reservation is the name of the
    new place. It is near a town—
    Fort Lauderdale. In the wars against
    Betty Mae's Seminole Ancestors,
    the fort was home to soldiers.

Betty Mae's family walks. They meet a train.
    They ride it. Then they walk some more.
    Betty Mae is tired when she reaches
    Dania Reservation.

Her dog, Jeep, is already there.
    Jeep nuzzles her: *Welcome home*.

t Dania the family keeps up many old ways. On shivering nights, sometimes by moonlight, Betty Mae eats oranges roasted by the camp's fire.

Her lessons are from Elders. In stories of the Little Turtle and the Wolf, Gray Bear, the Deer Girl, and more, they sing respect for the Breathgiver's creations. Betty Mae takes each story into her heart.

When visitors join the camp at night they marvel at the fire-lit sight. Rabbit beds down with dog, who is cuddled into cat.

Says Ada Tiger, a skillful hunter:
My Betty Mae can raise and tame anything.

11

Seminole men prepare a garden among trees, in a traditional way.

Ada Tiger and Mary Tiger plant guava, bananas, corn, and long Seminole pumpkins. Sugarcane stalks shoot up to the sky.

Betty Mae is a garden helper. For candy she snacks on the sugarcane.

As she helps, the women tell about the Corn Lady, the Witch Owls, the Little People, and How Little Dog Came to Be, stories from a time when all the animals talked.

Betty Mae helps find cedar, strangler fig, rattle box plant, frost weed, and Carolina willow. These are important for Tribal Medicine.

She even learns to help medicine women bring new life at birthing time.

A growing Betty Mae hears Mission words from an Oklahoma Seminole spoken about the One who can lead the wolf to lie with the lamb. Betty Mae won't skin a rabbit for the cook-fire stew. She never holds a rifle to learn to shoot.

She plants her hands on her hips and says: *Every living thing has a purpose, and that's not to make it dead.*

n a Mission trip to Oklahoma, Betty Mae's 13-year-old eyes grow wide. She watches a girl laugh, just from looking at drawings with letters on paper.

What is that? Betty Mae demands.

It talks to you, her new friend says. Betty Mae stares at the paper with pictures—a comic book. She looks at it this way and that. The paper with pictures doesn't talk to Betty Mae. Is this a trick?

The girl tells Betty Mae, *I'm reading.*

Betty Mae asks, *What's reading?*

The girl says, *It's something you do in school.*

ack at home, Betty Mae tells her grandmother, *I want to go to school. I want to go to school.*

Betty Mae sings as she stirs the corn sofki.
I want to go to school.

Betty Mae pleads with Elders when she picks pumpkins.
I want to go to school.

Betty Mae prays to the Breathgiver before she falls asleep.
I want to go to school.

Betty Mae is 14. She wears her first store-bought dress. She wiggles toes trapped inside leather, her first shoes.

The Cherokee Indian Boarding School is where Betty Mae lives and learns. People of a faith called Quaker, the Society of Friends, are some of the teachers.

She likes to learn. But she misses her people. In the snow-chilled mountain air, Betty Mae takes her warmth from memories. She tells stories about swamp custard apple trees, alligator mamas floating babies on their backs, orchids, cabbage palms, her tamed tall crane, and her dog, Jeep, who always tugged her home from the dangers of the woods.

In her first school year, Betty Mae advances to fourth grade. In the next year she skips ahead two more grades. To finish her education, she moves on to Kiowa Teaching Hospital, in Lawton, Oklahoma. She tells of people back home without inside bathrooms, without clean water.

She trains in nursing for two years,
     refusing to get sick at the sight of surgery,
     working night and day. Betty Mae stands
     straight under a starched white cap.

ow she can pick a job from anywhere in the Indian Nation. She remembers her mother Ada Tiger's work as a Medicine Woman. Despite joys, she saw babies dying from fevers, measles, and worms. She remembers that her baby sister died of whooping cough at the tender age of three.

Betty Mae returns home to work with the people she loves on the land she loves.

Nurse Betty Mae drives a dark sedan as part of a visiting clinic crew. Now she walks into a camp deep in the Everglades. A gun comes into view. The man with the gun says: *Stop! We've got Indian medicine. We don't need you.*

The nurses drive a little bit away. Soon a grandmother with babies, a mother with children, aunts with nephews, slip out to meet them.

Women walk back to camp with new medicine tucked among long folds of patchwork skirts. They trust Nurse Betty Mae.

Beautiful Betty Mae Tiger marries
Moses Jumper, of the Panther clan,
a handsome Navy warrior who
volunteered on the U.S.S. *Lexington*,
a ship set on fire in World War II.

The nursing job pays little. Betty Mae also
sells crafts at the *Jungle Queen* boat
landing, where tourists visit. Her husband
works there, too. He is the star alligator
wrestler for Captain Al Starts.

On days when her husband is sick, Betty Mae
climbs into that alligator pit.

The tourist job can't be lost.

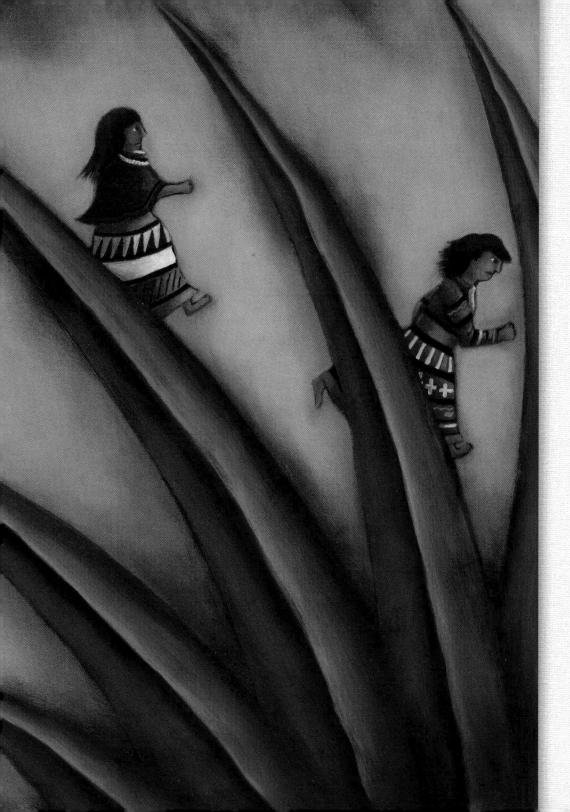

etty Mae is everywhere for her Tribe.
In the middle of a field, school
children hear an engine. Here is Mrs.
Jumper. She makes them clean up
and takes them back to school.
She finds truant children wherever
they hide, in buildings or in the woods.

She tells them the story of how she begged to
learn to read, how she pleaded
with the Elders:
I want to go to school.

It is a time of change for Betty Mae's people. A big highway divides the land. A language surrounds them that most adult Seminoles and many children can't read or write—English.

Many people live under cabbage palm roofs, without clean water or electricity. The U.S. government asks the Seminoles to organize a Tribal government, one that will work with the leaders of Washington, D.C.

Betty Mae travels throughout the Everglades, where families live, interpreting in two Seminole languages—Creek and Mikasuki. Working with the people to represent their choice, she helps set up a Tribal Council in 1957.

She helps start *Seminole Indian News* in 1961, written by Miccosukee and Seminole people. She is an interpreter in courtrooms and emergency rooms.

She is a voice for her people.

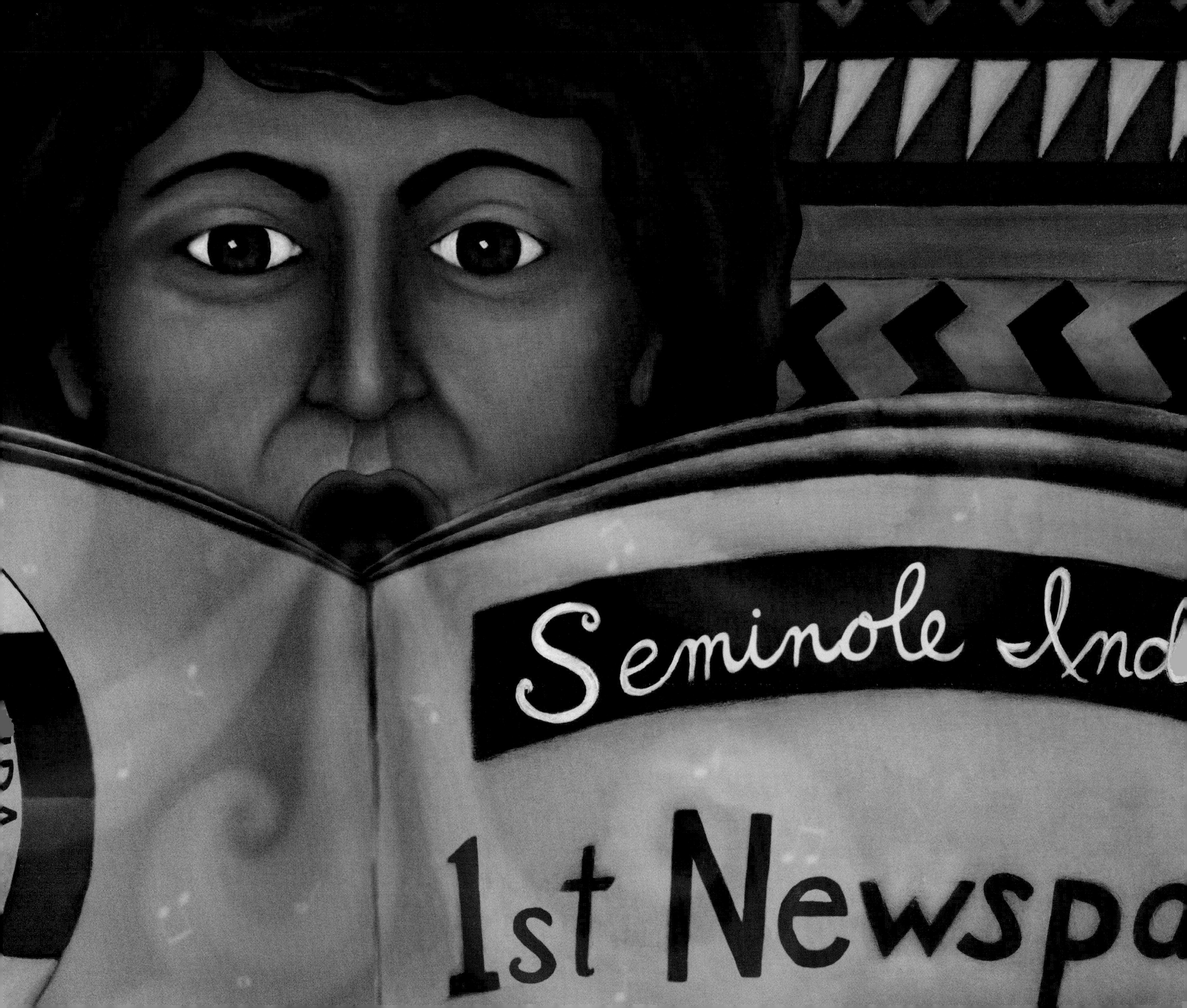
Seminole Ind
1st Newspa

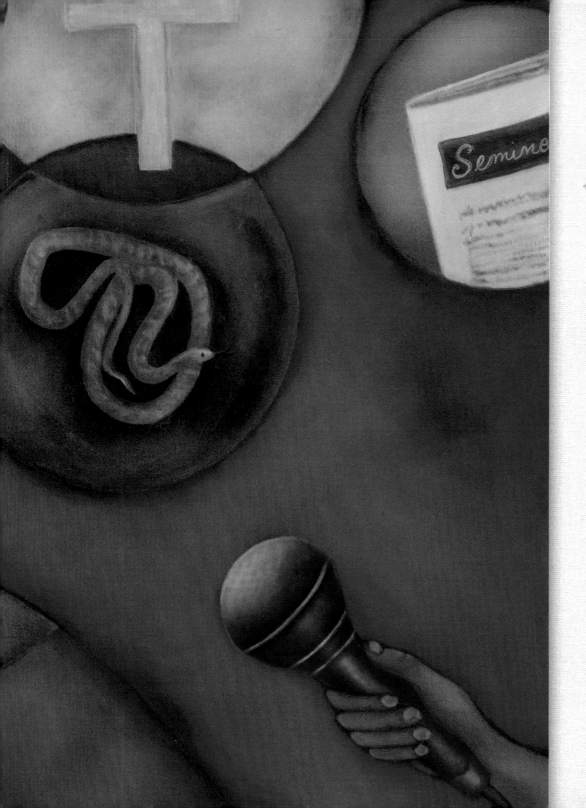

Betty Mae asks her people to elect her as their leader. For ten years, Tribal chairmen of the Seminole government she helped create have all been men. There is talk about her break with some traditional beliefs. There is talk about her Mission faith.

One night in May of 1967, when the votes tally up, there are 116 votes for her opponent. But Betty Mae receives 170. A woman has won! The Seminole Tribe has elected one of the first female tribal leaders in modern times. Betty Mae gives interviews to city newspapers. She is making good news for her people.

The baby who Tribal Elders wanted to throw away in the swamp is now the leader of her people.

*L*eader Betty Mae still sings her stories and
remembers the old ways. Storytelling,
sewing, and songs are part of the first
Seminole Fair.

She sits by soft piles of tribal patchwork,
fabric rainbows of the Everglades.

In the festival circle she tells stories sung
to her when she swayed in the sleep
hammock on fire-lit nights. She tells
of the Corn Lady, the Twins, the Witch
Owls, the Little People, the Deer Girl,
Little Frog, How Little Dog Came To Be,
stories of greed, stealth, health, and speed,
of panther, rabbit, swamp mice, and snake,
from the time when all the animals talked.

Those who listen to her imagine the
gigantic 'glades near the end of land.
Are these stories just tales
to pass the time?

Not so, says Betty Mae Tiger Jumper:
*These are the stories that showed us
how to live.*

AFTERWORD

"The oak remembered distinctly those men and women of the past…" — from *"The Council Oak,"* a poem by Moses Jumper, Jr.

Estonko ("hello") to the children; I have many good stories about my mother, Betty Mae Tiger Jumper, one of the strongest people I have ever known. One involves a bicycle. I was four days too young to begin school with all my reservation friends in 1957. So with the help of a scholarship, my mother started me in a private school, 13 miles away from our home.

One morning our truck broke down. I thought there would be no school for me that day. But my mother found a bicycle, held it steady, and told me to climb up on the handlebars. So picture us: My mother in her traditional Seminole patchwork long skirt, pedaling a bicycle along the road with me balanced in front. We didn't get very far before we accepted a ride from a friend who saw us near the highway traffic. This shows you how determined my mother was about anything important to her in her world. And education for children was always very, very important to her.

I am pleased you have decided to read this special story about the amazing life of Betty Mae Tiger Jumper and about our proud people. Know that lessons I learned from mother and grandmother have helped me through life. I hope you learn important lessons that will help you always. *Sho na´ bish* ("Thank you").

MOSES JUMPER, JR.

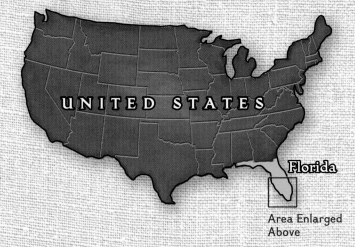

Area Enlarged Above

CHRONOLOGY

1513
As many as 200,000 Natives in various tribes, none known as Seminole, thrive on the peninsula now known as Florida.

Spain claims the area as La Florida.

1813–1814
Creek Indian War, Alabama. Gen. Andrew Jackson's takeover of Native lands sends families (later called Seminoles) to seek shelter in Florida Territory.

1818–1842 & circa 1855–58
Battles and guerilla warfare during three U.S. attempts to vanquish the Seminoles

1833 or after
In North Florida young female ancestors of Betty Mae Jumper escape brutal guards during forced eviction to the Territory of Oklahoma. Guided by the stars, they journey home to Jupiter, Florida.

1845
Territory of Florida becomes the 27th U.S. state.

1860
Mary Tustenuggee Gopher Tiger, Betty Mae's grandmother, is born.

circa 1883
Ada Tiger, Betty Mae's mother, is born.

1890s–early 1900s
Mary Tustenuggee Tiger runs 75 head of cattle, and also keeps horses and hogs.

1923-1928
Betty Mae Tiger born and raised outdoors at Indiantown Seminole Camp, Florida.

circa 1928
Threats against Betty Mae, age 5, cause her family to move near Fort Lauderdale, Florida.

1936
Betty Mae sees Juanita Tiger's comic book in Oklahoma and wants to learn to read.

circa 1937
Betty Mae begins school in winter snow, Cherokee, North Carolina, at age 14.

1945
Betty Mae graduates from Kiowa Teaching Hospital, Oklahoma, with cousin Agnes Parker.

1940s
Tribal Elder holds gun on Nurse Betty Mae, ordering her away from remote camp.

1946
Betty Mae Tiger of the Snake clan, and Moses Jumper of the Panther clan, marry.

She continues to work as a nurse, starts to sell crafts, and also wrestles alligators when Moses can't.

1947, 1951, & after
The Jumpers have 2 children: Rebecca Ann and Moses, Jr., and raise two more children, Boettner and Scarlett Marie.

1947 & after
Betty Mae called "Doctor Lady" in nursing work

She works as a volunteer interpreter for families

1957
Betty Mae travels in South Florida to help create and serve on first Seminole Tribal Council.

1961
Betty Mae and Alice Joy Osceola, Miccosukee Tribe, begin first Seminole newspaper, the *Seminole Indian News.*

1962
The Miccosukee Tribe officially organizes. These South Florida people have a traditional cultural history and a language, Mikasuki, that some Seminoles also speak.

1967
Betty Mae is elected Seminole Tribal Chairman.

1983
Betty Mae begins editing the *Seminole Tribune;* wins awards.

1970s
Home fire destroys Betty Mae's important papers and keepsakes.

Betty Mae named an advisor to President Richard M. Nixon on Indian matters.

1994
Betty Mae wins Florida Folk Heritage Award.

She receives Doctor of Humane Letters, Florida State University.

Betty Mae's book for all ages, *Legends of the Seminoles,* is published.

Late 1990s to present
She battles cancer.

Betty Mae Jumper arrives online at www.semtribe.com and receives worldwide fan mail from all ages.

MORE ABOUT BETTY MAE TIGER JUMPER

YOUNG BETTY MAE

Betty Mae always wanted to know more about her Frenchman father, a trader and trapper named Abe Barton, but that was not to be.

At her birth, women, including a white woman named Elizabeth "Sis" Savage, attended her mother, Ada Tiger. They were in a special open-air birthing *chickee (chikit)*, or hut, made of poles and palm fronds, near the Indiantown Seminole camp in South Florida, circa April 1923.

Betty Mae's grandmother, Mary Tustenuggee Gopher Tiger, taught her the Mikasuki (also called Hitchiti) language and her Great-uncle Jimmie Gopher, whom she called Grandpa, taught her to speak Creek (also called Muscogee). Her grandfather was Capt. Tom Tiger, a powerful medicine man who greeted Chester A. Arthur, the U.S. President, during his Okeechobee, Florida area fishing trip in 1883. Tiger's granddaughter Betty Mae would grow up to accept a committee appointment from another President, Richard M. Nixon.

By 12 years old, bilingual Betty Mae (speaking Mikasuki/Hitchiti and Creek/Muscogee) had also picked up enough words to communicate in a language foreign to her—English. But she didn't know how to read or write it. Of her unyielding desire to leave her people and add a non-Native education to her skills, she said: "My grandmother was sure I'd come to harm mingling with whites, as the women in her family had. She thought the only fit life for an Indian girl was helping her with her corn, beans, and pumpkin garden until I married."

When she was home on a break from her education, Betty Mae and a friend were refused sit-down service at a Fort Lauderdale, Florida, store lunch counter. She left and talked to local officials about this discrimination. This resulted in a local politicians' intervention. Later, they returned and were served a sandwich, seated. But they had proved their point and left the food and drink uneaten.

When Betty Mae finished high school, she and her cousin Agnes Parker were the first of the Florida Seminole Tribe to do so. By 1954, only five Seminoles had graduated. Betty Mae worked as a traveling nurse between remote Seminole camps, often unpaid. She fixed her car's flat tires in wild places. She carried a machete in case of rattlesnakes. Eventually she was able to treat families whose elders had first held a rifle on her. Families knew she had saved their babies' lives. They thanked her with gifts of cured game, fruit, and vegetables. They called her "Doctor Lady."

As Chairman of her Tribe, Mrs. Jumper directed a four-man council. She told an interviewer in 1967, the year she was first elected Chairman: "It's a challenge. Women have never held political office in Indian tribes." Eventually, she was a leader in a four-tribe coalition.

Betty Mae Tiger Jumper and Moses Jumper raised four children. Moses Jumper, Sr. died in December 1992. Betty Mae Tiger Jumper has published three books: *And With the Wagon Came God's Word; Legends of the Seminoles,* written with Peter B. Gallagher; and *A Seminole Legend: The Life of Betty Mae Tiger Jumper,* with Patsy West. Betty Mae is the subject of *The Corn Lady,* a storytelling video, and she appears on *Beautiful Beyond,* from The National Museum of the American Indian and The Smithsonian Folkways' *Heartbeat: Voices of First Nations Women,* a compilation of Native American women's music.

A modern medical clinic on the Dania/Hollywood, Florida Seminole Reservation is named in Betty Mae's honor. She holds the first Lifetime Achievement Award from the Native American Journalist's Association; Native American Indian Women's Association honors; an Honorary Doctorate from Florida State University; Florida Women's Hall of Fame honors; and the Florida Folk Life Heritage Award, among many others.

WHY I WROTE THIS STORY

One reason I wrote this story begins in Sarasota, Florida, when I was about 15 and my mother handed me a newspaper article. It showed a beautiful photograph of a woman with dark wavy hair and a long rainbow-colored skirt. The story told how she had just been the first female elected leader of the unconquered Seminole Tribe of Florida. "This is very important," my mother told me. I read it and kept it. About 15 years later I was assigned to write about a Native American festival for a newspaper. I came upon a table stacked like others with brilliant Seminole Indian patchwork clothing. But what caught my eye at the end of the table was a stack of newspapers. I picked one up and read. "You can have it. It's free," a woman said to me after awhile. I hadn't noticed her as she sat on a folding chair behind piles of the clothing. But now a shiver of recognition ran through me. "Oh my, you're Betty Mae Jumper!" I said. "I'm so glad to meet you." We chatted for a long time that day. After that I began to read her newspaper regularly, continuing my education about her life story and the story of her proud people from Georgia and Alabama, who adapted to the Big Cypress Swamp and Everglades.

~jga

GLOSSARY

Native words listed are from two languages not traditionally written, Creek (also called Muscogee) and Mikasuki (also Miccosukee). Sources include: *Legends of the Seminole; The Seminole Tribe of Florida; A Guide to Miccosukee Language; A Seminole Legend;* and a museum catalog, *"Seminole People of Florida: Survival & Success."*

BREATHGIVER In the Seminole creation belief, the Breathgiver, also Breathmaker, trapped animals inside Earth. The creatures later burst out, when tree roots dug into the ground.

CABBAGE PALM The state tree of Florida. Source of palm fronds for basket-making, fiber for both fire-starting and dolls for tourists, and the trunk for chickee posts. They are also cut down to prepare the heart of palm vegetable dish. *See p. 8, the palm with the scraggly trunk.*

CHEKE/ CHICKEE/ CHIKIT Open to-the-air, palm-thatched building for sleeping, eating, work (such as sewing), and sometimes even cooking. *See p. 4, p. 6-7, p. 11, p. 15, p. 19, p. 31, p. 32.*

CIRCA Used to qualify a date, meaning around or near in time

CLANS Family groups, according to the mother's side of the family. Some clan names are Panther, Wind, Bird, Bear, Deer, Snake, Bigtown, and Otter. Betty Mae Tiger Jumper is from the Snake Clan.

CREEK (MUSCOGEE) One of the two traditional languages of the Seminole people

EVERGLADES/ OLD EVERGLADES Historically, a shallow water flow from Lake Okeechobee, moving east and south. Much larger than Everglades National Park, which contains just a portion of the Everglades. Today people actually live on drained land that was once part of Old Everglades.

HO-LA-WA-GUS A word meaning bad luck; what the Elders said Betty Mae got from her father.

LITTLE PEOPLE A legend says that thousands of little people live in the holes of trees, which is why lightning strikes trees, to get at the little people.

MEMORY A people's history without written language, Memory includes the passing down of information from Elders to the next generation.

MICCOSUKEE A tribe in South Florida with a traditional cultural history similar to the Seminoles. Their traditional language is Mikasuki/ Hitchiti. The Miccosukee Tribe officially organized separately from the Seminoles.

MIKASUKI (HITCHITI) One of the two traditional languages of the Seminole people

PALMETTO/ SAW PALMETTO A shrub and sometimes a tree with tooth-edged palm fronds used for making baskets and fans. Also valued for berries used in medicine. *See front cover, front flap, endpapers, title page, p. 4-5, p. 7, p. 8-9, p. 10-11, p. 13, p. 20-21, p. 24-25, p. 32-33.*

PATCHWORK DESIGNS Patterns on traditional clothing (never called costumes). These patterns include rain, lightning, fire, broken arrow, man on horse, bird, the four directions, crawfish, tree, rattlesnake, and bones.

SEDAN Betty Mae remembered driving with another visiting nurse to remote Indian family camps, using a sedan, a type of car. *See p. 20.*

SEMINOLE The agreed spelling of a traditional term, *simano-li,* for the people the Spanish said were *cimarron,* which describes plants and animals that are wild or runaway. The Museum of Florida History says when used to describe a people, the word, Seminole, can also be thought to mean, pioneer.

SLEEP HAMMOCK A bed made by hanging a blanket or fabric from rope strung between cypress poles in a chickee. *See p. 7.*

SOFKEE/ SOFKI An important drink or soup made from corn. It was kept available at the campfire to feed any arriving family member or invited guest, day or night. *See p. 15.*

SWAMP CUSTARD APPLE TREE A swamp-loving tree with yellow-green flowers and fruit. Called alligator apple, since gators eat them, and pond apple, since it likes to be in water.

TRUANT Betty Mae found children who were truant, or missing from school without permission, and brought them back to school. *See p. 24-25.*

Go online for more information on these native languages.
www.seminoletribe.com/culture/
   language.shtml
www.native-languages.org/mikasuki
www.native-languages.org/creek

SELECTED BIBLIOGRAPHY

Preparations to write this story included my visits to the Ah-Tah-Thi-Ki Museum, Big Cypress; the Seminole Okalee Indian Village, Hollywood, FL; The Museum of the American Indian, Washington, D.C.; and The Museum of Florida History, Tallahassee, FL, special exhibit, "Seminole People of Florida: Survival & Success." Other resources I drew upon include:

• Author interviews and conversations with Betty Mae Tiger Jumper: at the Tallahassee Jr. Museum, early 1980s; in travel with BMTJ from Hollywood, FL, to Miami Beach, for "Evening of Storytelling: Eight Women of Florida's Past," at the Sanford L. Ziff Jewish Museum of Florida, March 12, 1995; at the Seminole Tribune office, Hollywood, FL, June 23, 1999; at the Jumper residence, Hollywood, FL, December 5, 2001.

• Blackard, David. Patchwork and Palmettos. Fort Lauderdale, FL: Fort Lauderdale Historical Society, 1990.

• Braman, Arlette N. and Bill Helin. Traditional Native American Arts & Activities. New York: John Wiley & Sons, 2000.

• Cerulean, Susan, ed. The Book of the Everglades. Minneapolis, MN: Milkweed Editions, 2002.

• Downs, Dorothy. Patchwork: Seminole and Miccosukee Art and Activities. Sarasota, FL: Pineapple Press, 2005.

• "Women of Legend." FHC Forum, Vol. XXXI, No. 1 (2007).

• Garbarino, Merwyn S. Big Cypress: A Changing Seminole Community. Chicago: Holt, Rinehart and Winston, 1972.

• Glenn, James Lafayette. My Work Among the Florida Seminoles. Gainesville, FL: University Press of Florida, 1982.

• Green, Rayna. Women in American Indian Society. New York: Chelsea House, 1992.

• Jumper, Betty Mae. "So Near Heaven and Agnes," Hollywood, FL: Seminole Tribune, Vol. XX, No. 28.

• Jumper, Betty Mae Tiger, and Patsy West. A Seminole Legend: The Life of Betty Mae Tiger Jumper. Gainesville, FL: University Press of Florida, 2001.

• Jumper, Betty Mae, Peter B. Gallagher, and Guy LaBree. Legends of the Seminoles. Sarasota, FL: Pineapple Press, 1994.

• Jumper, Betty Mae. "57th Anniversary of the First Seminole Baptist Church." Seminole Tribune, Vol. XV, No. 21.

• Jumper, Betty Mae. "Lak Ka Che Hoo Mashe Ahfachkee," Seminole Tribune, Vol. XX, No. 19.

• "Gripping Story of the Seminoles." St. Augustine Record. Oct. 27, 2001.

• Miccosukee Tribe of Indians of Florida, A Guide to the Miccosukee Language. Miami, FL: 1978, 1996.

• "She Bridges Two Ways of Life," St. Petersburg (FL) Times. September 22, 1967.

• West, Patsy. The Enduring Seminoles: From Alligator Wrestling to Casino Gaming. Gainesville, FL: University Press of Florida, 2008.

• West, Patsy. The Seminole and Miccosukee Tribes of Florida. Columbia, SC: Arcadia Publishing, 2002.

• Wickman, P.R. "State Awards Highest Folklife Honor to Tribune Editor, Tribal Leader, Betty Mae Jumper." Seminole Tribune, Vol. XVII, No. 1.

• Weisman, Brent Richards. Unconquered People: Florida's Seminole and Miccosukee Indians. Gainesville, FL: University Press of Florida, 1999.

TO EXPLORE MORE

The Seminole Tribe of Florida (www.seminoletribe.com) operates the Ah-Tah-Thi-Ki Museum (www.ahtahthiki.com), the first tribally governed museum in the U.S. to receive national accreditation from the American Association of Museums. The Seminole Tribe is also represented in the National Museum of the American Indian (www.nmai.org).

To learn about Everglades National Park and Big Cypress National Preserve, see www.nps.gov/ever and www.nps.gov/bicy.

Florida's Miccosukee Tribe, closely related to the Seminoles, can also be found online at www.miccosukee-seminolenation.com. The western Seminole Nation of Oklahoma is at www.seminolenation.com.

IN MEMORY OF MY PARENTS, WHO SHARED A LOVE OF ORAL HISTORY IN STORIES THEY TOLD; ALSO IN GRATITUDE FOR MY MOTHER'S CLIPPING OF A NEWSPAPER STORY ABOUT THE HISTORIC SEMINOLE TRIBAL ELECTION.

~jga

FOR MY MOM, ANOTHER AMAZING WOMAN.

~ld

Many appreciations flow from my heart for: Betty Mae Tiger Jumper and her family, especially Moses Jumper, Jr., poet and author of *Echoes in the Wind*; LaQuita Jumper; the memory of Winifred Tiger; family members who prefer privacy; Phyllis Buster; the many Seminole Ancestors before Betty Mae Tiger Jumper whose stories of bravery are kept by Memory, and those today working to keep Memory: The Seminole Tribe of Florida; Virginia Mitchell; The *Seminole Tribune*; the generous staff of the Ah-Tah-Thi-Ki Museum, especially Tina Osceola, Anne McCudden, Diana Stone, and Pedro Zepeda; Geneva Shore; David Blackard; Dr. Patricia R. Wickman; Patsy West; Dr. Joe Knetsch and also Linda Drexel Knetsch, sharp-eyed reader since Riverview *Ram Page* days; Demelza Champagne, National Museum of the American Indian, Smithsonian Institution; Joe Quetone, Governor's Council on Indian Affairs; The Museum of Florida History, especially Kieran Orr, Linda Humphrey, and Susan Stratton; Larry Coltharp; Joan Morris; Florida Memory Project and Florida Archives, Secretary of State Kurt S. Browning's office; Jody Taylor and The Laura Jepsen Institute; Florida Humanities Council; Michael Gannon, esteemed University of Florida history professor; UF Samuel Proctor Oral History Program and P. K. Yonge Library of Florida History, University of Florida; Susan Cerulean, for loan of "the wild heart of Florida" phrase; Dorothy Downs; Rose-anne Reanier; Emily Rosen; Joan Broerman; Erin Turner; Megan Hiller; Atlantic Center for the Arts; Ann Brady; Michael Dirda; Myra Forsberg; Paolo Annino, Anna Annino; Lisa Desimini; and Nancy Feresten, Jennifer Emmett, David M. Seager, Rebecca Baines, Felita Vereen-Mills, and Priyanka Lamichhane, Lori Renda, Grace Hill, Carl Mehler, Jennifer Eaton, Kathryn Murphy, and Susan Donnelly at National Geographic. I thrive on the regular meetings at my house of sharp critique partners Ann Morrow, Debra Katz, and M.R. Street.

~jga

Photo on page 36 courtesy Louis Capron Collection, P.K. Yonge Library of Florida History, University of Florida.

Book design by David M. Seager.

Text copyright © 2010 by Jan Godown.
Illustrations copyright © 2010 by Lisa Desimini.
Cover copyright © 2010 by National Geographic Society.
All rights reserved. Published by Scholastic Inc., 557 Broadway, New York, NY 10012, by arrangement with National Geographic Society.
Printed in the U.S.A.

ISBN-13: 978-0-545-62021-5
ISBN-10: 0-545-62021-X